Alex

BE STILL

The Power of Biblical Meditation

Thank you so much for coming to my workshop! I pray that this book is a blessing to you.

With gratitude,

JHENI SOLIS

This book is dedicated to my two greatest loves on earth,

Shawn Solis and Jade Solis

Table of Contents

Foreword
by
Lisa Washington

Meditation is a beautiful way for us to center our minds and connect with our Creator. Not only does meditation help center ourselves to connect with God, but it also reduces stress, lengthens attention span, promotes emotional health and may reduce age-related memory loss. So why do we not put much focus on meditation in our Christian walks?

When we hear the word meditation – especially as Christians – we can find ourselves in a space of fear, judgement or even a lack of understanding. The culture of meditation can contribute to such feelings. The word meditation is not used often in our Christian culture, but we do see it being practiced throughout the Bible; Even the word itself is mentioned in the scriptures.

The definition is simple, and whether or not we use the term "meditate," we practice it daily. The word meditation comes from the Latin word meditārī, which has a range of meanings including to reflect on, to study and to practice.

"One evening as he was walking and meditating in the fields, he looked up and saw the camels coming." - Genesis 24:63

"My mouth will speak words of wisdom; the meditation of my heart will give you understanding." - Psalm 49:3

What I love about *BE STILL: The Power of Biblical Meditation* is how my dear friend Jheni has made meditation a place where we can clear the clutter and connect with Him which is what I believe God has intended it to be from the beginning. Jheni's many years of experience in Yoga, Ayurveda, Meditation and Energy Science has allowed her to birth a powerful, yet extremely approachable "how-to" meditation book. This book is informative, practical and very inspiring. As I moved through each page, exercise and meditative technique, I felt as if I was on a journey of awakening and finding a deeper way to connect to God. She takes you on a beautiful spiritual retreat in the privacy of your own home.

BE STILL: The Power of Biblical Meditation is a book that you will find yourself going back to again and again.

Lisa Washington,
Author, Chef, Yogi, Motivational Speaker, Life Coach,
CEO of B'Tyli Wellness and Beauty Co.

Acknowledgements

Thank you, God, for being my Father in Heaven. Thank you for creating me and having big dreams for me even before I knew what my dreams were. Thank you for putting this book on my heart 3 years ago. Thank you for being patient with me while I worked through my insecurities, procrastination and doubts to finally write this book. Thank you for speaking to me and listening to me every day.

Thank you, Jesus, for being the Lord of my life since 2004. Thank you for your ultimate sacrifice that made me worthy to be saved, all because of your blood of atonement. Thank you that even if I was the only one that needed saving, you would still have gone to the cross. Thank you that I can live a life of freedom in Your name.

Thank you, Holy Spirit, for speaking to me every day. You are the essence of God, the energy that moves through space and time. You are my biblical-moral compass. You are the One who puts certain people on my heart. You are the One who reminds me of Jesus' Lordship in my life. You are the One who changes the desires of my heart to line up with God's desires for me. Thank you for residing within me as a deposit guaranteeing my place in Heaven.

Thank you, Shawn, my amazing husband. I thank God every day that I get to be your wife and your best friend. I am so grateful for how you support my dreams, no matter how crazy it may sound. Thank you for being the calm in my storm, the yin to my yang, and for setting an example of godliness in our household. I love you more today than yesterday.

Thank you, Jade, my sweet daughter. I feel so blessed to have you not only as my daughter, but also as one of my best friends, road trip partner, shopping buddy, sister in Christ, and one of my biggest supporters. My heart is filled with joy to have you as the cover model of this book! Thank you for loving me without judgment. Your constant desire to please God inspires me. I love you with all my heart.

Thank you, dad (Richard Yoon), for passing on the gift of writing to me. You have always accepted and loved me even when you didn't understand or agree with my dreams and decisions. I will always treasure the 31 years that I got to have you as my father on earth. I love you and I miss you every day.

Thank you, mom (Nancy Yoon), for pushing me to be a better version of myself. Thank you for all the sacrifices you've made to provide me with opportunities that you didn't have growing up. Your inner strength inspires me to search for my own authentic inner strength. I love you.

Thank you, my big brother (Daniel Yoon), for who you are. I respect you so much for all your accomplishments in life. You're such a wonderful brother, and I'm grateful for how much you go out of your way to make me feel welcome whenever I come for a visit. I love you.

Thank you, my In-Laws (Yolanda Fabela, Danny & Angie Solis, Julia Yoon, Michael & Danielle Solis, Eric Solis & Dennis Caasi, and all of my extended Families-In-Law), for loving me as if I were related by blood. Your love and support throughout the years have meant the world to me. I love you all.

Thank you, Crystal Mbanuzue, for holding me accountable to make this book happen! I'm so grateful for your friendship and sisterhood. Thank you for challenging my heart in ways that I don't want to be challenged (but so badly need). Thank you for taking me to the emergency room in Myrtle Beach. Thank you for always being there when it really counts. You're a true friend through and through.

Thank you, Leslie Price, my best friend. You have taught me so much about listening to the Spirit, loving God and people wholeheartedly, humility... and how to be a true friend. You are everything I am not, and I thank God every day for bringing you into my life when my family and I moved to North Carolina in 2015.

Thank you, Brooke Kidwell, Lavonia Drabot and Jennifer Fuller, for being the women's ministry leaders that think outside the box in Christianity which allows me to explore my authenticity in Christ.

Thank you, Rebecca Hoke, for our talk in 2018. Your support and excitement for this book has allowed me to take a dream and make it a reality.

Thank you, Amy Dohlman, Bev Wacker, Ched & Marvie Dumancas, Christine Famularo, Cristina Vargas, Dawn Mercer, Gail Allen, Jill Jaquez, Lia Shytle, Marcus Johnson, Melina Ryter, Sydney Diggs, Tina Ames and Twanda Williams for always creating a safe place for me to share my heart without feeling judged.

Thank you, Ron Drabot, Rodney Fuller, Tim Kidwell, Uchenna Mbanuzue, Derik & Leigh Anne Vett, Mark & Connie Mancini, Todd & Patti Asaad, Paul & Yoly Avila and Will & Addy Garcia, for your example of leadership through servanthood.

Thank you, The Charlotte Church (NC), DFW Church (TX) and The Valley Church (CA) for your love and support throughout my life as a disciple of Jesus Christ.

Thank you, Lisa Washington, my spirit sister. You embody true authenticity in Christ. Your excitement for life inspires me beyond words. I am so blessed to have you in my life. I feel honored to have you as one of the models in this book. Thank you so much for being my mentor, sister in Christ, a true friend and confidante.

Thank you, Keegan Leiba, for your friendship and vulnerability. Thank you for setting an example of pursuing the dreams that God has set in your heart.

Thank you, Kristina Millsaps, for allowing me photograph you for this book; your God-given beauty and poise have elevated it beyond my dreams! I'm grateful for your friendship and sisterhood.

Thank you, Shanon Buffington. The training I received from you has allowed me to discover my dharma.

I wouldn't be who I am today without all of you. I love you all.

Introduction

What I am about to share with you is not some hidden secret, unattainable by the general population... because frankly, I am the general population; However, what I do have − and I'm so excited to share with you − is the experience and knowledge that I've acquired through close to two thousand hours of studying and training in Yoga, Ayurveda, Meditation and Energy Science as well as many years of learning at the feet of some amazing Bible Teachers and Ministers who have planted churches, have been on mission teams all over the world, served tirelessly in helping strengthen the spiritually weak, and most importantly, have set an example of godly love, grace, mercy, servanthood and humility.

This book contains stories from my own life as well as stories about others who have inspired and encouraged me in my walk with God especially in relation to being still. Some names and minor information have been changed to protect their privacy, and the names of public figures have been referenced without any changes. The end of each chapter (other than the first chapter) contains simple techniques to calm your mind and become still so that you can begin to practice meditation, working towards the goal of being still, followed by questions that will help you journal about your experiences with God.

All of the scriptures that I have referenced – but have not quoted – within the chapters can be found at the end of this book under "Scripture References."

In addition, the audio recordings for all of the meditation, relaxation and breath control techniques can be found on my website, under the page called "Resources." (https://www.jhenisolis.com/resources) Password: **Psalm4610**.

I encourage you to take at least a few days in each chapter – instead of zipping right through the entire book – in order to ponder over the concepts which will allow yourself to experience a sense of transformation and insight.

I hope you enjoy reading this book, and I pray that you will bask in the unexplainable joy and peace that comes from learning to be still.

Prologue

"Be still and know that I am God."

What?

"Be. Still. And. Know. That. I. Am. God."

This is the first part of Psalm 46:10. As a Christian, I've heard this quoted by others and by the Holy Spirit numerous times. If you were to ask me what this means, my first interpretation would have probably been that in order for you to know who God truly is, you must be still. But as I began to dig deeper within my soul for a more authentic answer, I started to dissect this statement:

"Be Still"

The Hebrew translation for "be still" is *rapha* which means to become limp or let drop. These two small words can be such a huge task for us human beings. The challenge given here is to allow ourselves to become limp and weak by moving away from trying to do things with our own strengths. Instead of holding on to our worries, our plans, and our situations, God commands us to open our hands and release control.

I once had a friend who explained the concept of "open fists" to me. He said, "It's like you want to hold on, tight-fisted, to everything that you're trying to control, but God wants us to surrender it all to him. So, you open your fists, denying yourself of your arrogance and pride, and you give it all to God."

"And"

Not "Or." And. In addition to. Not separate from the next command.

"Know"

There's a difference between knowing facts about someone (like a celebrity or a pro athlete) and KNOWING someone. When I was around 11 or 12 years old, I was "in love" with the actor Mackenzie Astin (he played the role of Andy Moffatt in the TV show Facts of Life). I knew that his parents are John Astin and Patty Duke, and I knew that he grew up in Westwood, CA. I also knew other random facts about him thanks to Teen Beat, Tiger Beat and other teen magazines. But I didn't KNOW him. I've never met him in person, I've never been at his house and I have never spoken to him on the phone. Even though I was in his fan club, he didn't know me and I didn't know him.

On the other hand, I met this gorgeous man in 2000. We met at a Teen Ministry 70's costume party while we were both chaperoning. We fell in love, got married, and we had a beautiful daughter named Jade.

This gorgeous, God-fearing husband of mine, Shawn, is my better half. He's the calm in my storm, and he is a humble man for the most part. But I can tell on his face when he's feeling defensive about a situation because certain parts of his face tense up. No one else can tell, but I can. That's because I KNOW him. And when I'm being stubborn, he knows how to gently call me out on it with love and grace. Because he KNOWS me.

Do you know about God like you know about a famous celebrity, or do you KNOW God intimately like you would a family member or a close friend?

"That"

This word introduces and expresses the next statement that follows the previous action. In this case: Be still and know THAT...

"I AM"

The phrase "I AM" is mentioned several times in the Bible. In Exodus 3:13-14, Moses asks God, *"If I come to the people of Israel and say to them, 'The God of your fathers has sent me to you,' and they ask me, 'What is his name?' what shall I say to them?"* God tells Moses to say to them, *"I AM WHO I AM,"* and that *"I AM has sent me to you."*

Because I am not a bible scholar or a theologian, I won't go into an in-depth explanation other than to tell you that "I AM" is built out of the same Hebrew word for YHWH (pronounced YAHWEH, which is recorded as God's actual name). If you're interested in learning more about this whole topic, there are some great articles on www.desiringgod.org by John Piper.

But let's just think about the meaning behind "I am." This is a phrase you use before introducing yourself or explaining your identity. When I say, "I am Jheni Solis," "I am a disciple of Christ," "I am married," "I am a mother," "I am a Yoga Teacher," etc., what I'm doing is introducing myself as I would like for you to know me. So, when God proceeds to introduce Himself, we better pay attention!

"God"

When you think of God, what do you think of? Do you think of His creations? His omnipotence? His omniscience? His omnipresence? His character? Perhaps you're feeling disconnected from Him, bitter towards Him, or maybe you're questioning His existence. Whatever thoughts and feelings you have, admit it to yourself and then take a breath:

Take a deep inhale through the nose as you allow your belly to expand, keeping your shoulders relaxed. Open your mouth gently and exhale the sound, "Ha"

Now let's begin this journey of stillness together.

CHAPTER 1:
Who, What, When, Where and Why

As a lover of journalism and a newspaper editor in college, I always ask the questions, "Who," "What," "When," "Where" and "Why" (also, "How?") in majority of situations that I encounter. I find that this is an easy way for me to organize the information being given to me in the most efficient way. In saying this, I'm sure you may be thinking that I'm a more logical and practical person; however, being that I'm also a musician, vocalist, performer and a dancer, people I meet generally assume that I'm the creative type. I am actually both.

I constantly crave a balance in creativity and logic/order. I find that I'm much happier and at peace when I feel a balance in both worlds. I first need to organize the information in order for my creativity to be unleashed. This is how God created me. When I feel out of balance, I feel disconnected emotionally, spiritually and physically to all aspects of my life. Now that you know a little bit about how my brain works, let's dive into the 5 W's of Meditation (we'll get into the "How" in Chapters 2-7).

Who: Who is the Creator of Meditation?

You guess it: GOD! God is the Creator of meditation!

Shortly after moving to Charlotte, NC in 2015, I invited a college-aged girl to church as I was leaving Panera Bread. She said she was a student at a Bible College and was very involved in the church that was affiliated with the school, and after a brief but pleasant chat about God and the Bible, I gave her my business card to keep in touch.

Later that evening, I received a message from her where she was expressing her deep concern for my salvation because she read on my website that I'm a meditation coach. She advised me to pray to God and not engage in meditation that she believed was not righteous. She referred to a scripture about how you can invite evil spirits to enter you (Matthew 12:44-45). She told me that I was on dangerous ground and that I needed to repent.

I must admit, my initial reaction was to get prideful and defensive (which is really the same thing). Instead, I took a step back and thanked God for her in prayer for her heart of boldness to stand for what she believed was for God's glory. I replied to her with a humbler heart than I otherwise would have before praying, and I thanked her for her concern. I also explained to her that meditation is absolutely biblical and that not all meditation is a "paganistic practice."

Just like anything in life, we can take something God created and make it not of God (i.e. – corruption in politics, religious organizations, corporations, etc.). The meditation she was referring to was not the meditation that I practice. The biblical meditation that I practice is to practice stillness in heart, mind, soul and strength as stated in Joshua 1:8; Psalm 1:1-2; Psalm 104:34.

What: What is Biblical Meditation?

So, what is the difference between biblical and unbiblical meditation? Here is a breakdown of steps:

- Biblical Meditation

  a) Practice sitting still without movement (physical discipline)

  b) Practice de-cluttering your mind (emotional and mental discipline)

  c) Practice stillness of your soul (spiritual discipline)

  d) Create a connection to God and experience being in God's presence (spiritual connection/intimacy)

- Unbiblical Meditation

  a) Practice sitting still without movement (physical discipline)

b) Practice decluttering your mind (emotional and mental discipline)

c) Practice stillness of your soul (spiritual discipline)

d) Experience whatever happens (opening the door to your spirit for anything to happen)

As you can see, the only difference in biblical meditation vs. unbiblical meditation is *intention*. The mind is a very powerful thing. Your mind has the ability to change your feelings, your perspectives, and your future.

When: When is the best time to meditate?

The answer to this question depends on each individual and their lifestyles, but anytime is the best time to meditate!

The benefit of meditating the first thing in the morning is that your brain is at its freshest and void of all of the stimulation it's about to experience in the day. It also helps to start your day out with a calm mind and a positive perspective while increasing your focus and motivation for the day.

The benefit of meditating in the middle of the day is that you can do a re-set on your day that may not necessarily be going smoothly. You can activate your Parasympathetic Nervous System in the middle of a stressful day by taking 10-15 minutes to meditate (see Figure 1.1 on the next page). Meditating in the evenings can provide you with the decompression you need from your busy day. Meditation also aids in better sleep, so evening meditation can be great for people who experience insomnia. I welcome you to try various times of the day to see what works best for you.

Figure 1.1

Sympathetic vs. Parasympathetic Nervous Systems

Sympathetic Nervous System (SNS) is the "fight or flight" response to stress. When SNS is activated, the body releases stress hormones which allow us to take whatever action necessary for self-preservation. Activating the SNS causes the digestive system to shut down and other organs and muscles to contract.

Parasympathetic Nervous System (PNS) is the "rest and digest" response to homeostasis. Activating the PNS allows the body and the mind to heal and restore for optimal health.

Where: Where should I meditate?

Ideally, you want to find a quiet place free of noise and visual distractions. This could be a corner in a room, a closet, backyard, etc. Outside in nature is also a great place to meditate as long as it's private and you can ensure you won't be distracted by people passing by or conversations that may be taking place within earshot. It also helps to make the location of your meditation consistently the same. Making a certain spot as your meditation place with God will help you to grow in consistency and depth of your meditation experience.

Why: Why should I meditate?

We live in an age of technology and instant gratification. We want what we want, when we want it. Although this convenience can seem like we're advancing in life, it comes with grave consequences.

Studies have shown that time spent on our smartphones (social media, instant messaging, lightning speed search engines, etc.) is causing our brains to become slow. We're firing up the left hemisphere of our brains more than our right, and this is causing a great neuro-imbalance.

When you meditate, you activate the right hemisphere of the brain which causes you to experience more peace, patience, joy, love and bliss (see Figure 1.2 below).

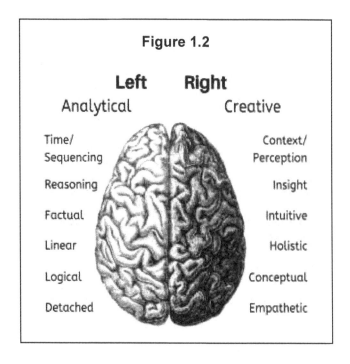

Figure 1.2

Left **Right**
Analytical Creative

Left	Right
Time/Sequencing	Context/Perception
Reasoning	Insight
Factual	Intuitive
Linear	Holistic
Logical	Conceptual
Detached	Empathetic

Meditating is also a way to create a path toward the atman. Atman, in Sanskrit[1], means *soul*. To experience the atman is to see the person you were created to be, before all of the life-baggage that you've acquired from others and from some of the unwise choices that you have made. The goal of meditation is to experience the presence of God and in turn, God shows you the purest essence of your soul. When you meet the atman, you will feel compelled to become more of that person, which is YOU in the purest form (see Figure 1.3 below).

Figure 1.3

In order to meet the Atman within you, you must do the work to peel off the layers that penetrate through these five sheaths/layers (known as *Koshas* in Sanskrit).

The first sheath is the physical layer that can be "peeled off" through physical movements such as yoga poses or general exercising. The second, third and fourth sheaths can be worked on through breath control practice and meditation. The fifth sheath can only be work on through meditation.

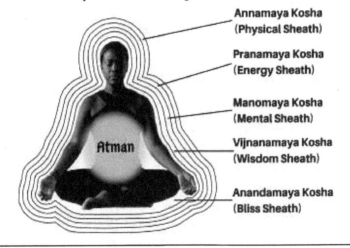

Annamaya Kosha
(Physical Sheath)

Pranamaya Kosha
(Energy Sheath)

Manomaya Kosha
(Mental Sheath)

Vijnanamaya Kosha
(Wisdom Sheath)

Anandamaya Kosha
(Bliss Sheath)

Atman

---

[1]*Sanskrit – Language of Ancient India from over 3500 years ago. Many Northern Indian Languages are derived from Sanskrit, and it is widely used in Yoga and Ayurveda.*

CHAPTER 2:
My First Savasana

I started dancing while I was attending preschool in Seoul, South Korea. It was part of their preschool program (they had a very structured and quite an extensive program in the arts as well as introduction to the academics), so dancing happened out of convenience. We learned ballet, interpretive dancing/movement, contemporary, and the traditional Korean dances. Fast forward to 6th grade; I enrolled in a ballet class at a local studio in Chatsworth, CA. I loved every minute of the tendus, pirouettes, and relevés... but I found myself always lingering after class to watch the jazz dancers. I would come home and try to do whatever I could remember from the jazz choreography I watched that day.

Eventually, I transitioned from ballet to jazz, which is where my true love of dance began. I fell so in love with dance that I was willing to do anything to become a professional dancer. At age 14, I decided to add Polynesian dancing to my repertoire as I learned the dances of Hawaii, Tahiti and New Zealand. Shortly afterwards, I was asked to join a professional Polynesian dance group.

Being a part of this professional dance group was how I learned to go after a passion. I would walk for an hour to dance rehearsals, and I would take the money I earned from gigs and used them to pay for dance-related expenses. After high school, I danced and choreographed for a number of concerts in California and Nevada.

Being a professional dancer made me feel like I was living my dream life; but it also left me with a lot of injuries. I started practicing Yoga as a way to rehabilitate my injured body.

Just like many people, I started practicing Yoga by watching and following instructions on a DVD. The challenge with practicing with a Yoga DVD is that it's almost impossible to know whether you're in proper alignment or not. In fact, it turned out that I had been doing certain poses with improper alignment for over a decade before I was made aware while I was going through a 200-Hour Yoga Teacher Training!

My first studio yoga experience was at a women's fitness and wellness spa in Northridge, CA that I was a member of at age 24. The yoga teacher was a gentle soul with great depth that shined in her eyes. I don't remember much from the class other than that during savasana, I felt a certain emotional and energetic release that left me on the verge of tears. I didn't understand what was happening at the time, but I came to realize that it was my body's way of releasing stuck emotions and energies that were hiding in the crevices of my soul. Even after such an incredible experience, my yoga practice continued to be sporadic and inconsistent; but I never forgot how I felt that day when I experienced my first real savasana.

Savasana, Sanskrit for "Corpse Pose," is the most challenging pose in Yoga because in our daily lives, we are constantly on the move. In this day in age of technology and multitasking, being still is considered to be a time-waster for the most part.

Even if we are able to physically stop moving, our minds are constantly thinking, problem-solving, organizing, worrying, rationalizing, irrationalizing, regretting and dwelling. And then there's the energetic and spiritual unsettling (the word energetics is referring to the movement of your spirit): Your environment, observations, and your DNA generally determines your energetic state (your tendency towards Type-A behaviors, your tendency towards being an introvert, and everything in between). So, even if you're able to become still physically and mentally, you have to somehow create an energetic and spiritual stillness. This is why savasana is such a challenging pose! But just like any yoga pose, it becomes easier with consistent practice. Savasana is a great place to begin the practice of being still which can be carried into a meditation practice.

TECHNIQUE:

Savasana

- Lie down on a comfortable but firm surface. Feel free to place a pillow under your head and under your knees if you'd like.

- Set the timer for 5 minutes (you may increase the time as you become more comfortable being still).

- Close your eyes and allow your feet to flop outward and the palms to face up, with fingers naturally curling in a little.

- Become aware of the breath. Allow the belly to rise and expand with each inhale; and with each exhale, allow the belly to gently return.

- Listen to the breath. Your breaths should be noiseless. You may intuitively hear the sound "So" at inhale and "Hum" at exhale.

- If any thoughts rise in your mind, imagine those thoughts melting away with each exhale.

- Once the timer goes off, roll over to your left side and stay there for a few breaths before using your arms to come up to a seated position.

JOURNALING PROMPTS:

1. What did you experience during your time of Savasana? Did you find it hard to lay still, or did you find yourself being able to relax immediately?

2. How would you be able to incorporate Savasana into your life for physical, mental, emotional, and spiritual benefits?

3. Write down any spiritual insights you may have received from God, and find scriptures that confirm these insights.

Mantra Practice

Mantra (मन्त्र) is Sanskrit for "energy-based sounds." All of God's creations have their own frequency of vibration, and all vibration has a sound. Mantras are unique sounds of God's creations. The modern, western world likes to refer to positive affirmations as mantras; however, the origin of mantra is based on the seed sound of each created entity. It is believed that when you recite/chant certain mantras, you begin to raise your own frequency of vibration to match that particular mantra (which is very favorable to our mind, body and spirit).

OM/AUM

The "OM/AUM" mantra is the most powerful mantra in my opinion. This mantra is the cumulative sound of all creation. I imagine it to be the sound that we make when we as humans, animals, earth, sea, and the entire universe collectively praise God.

- Get into a comfortably seated position.
    - Ideally, you want to be sitting on the floor with your legs crossed or kneeling using a pillow, bolster or a meditation cushion to create a neutral spinal alignment, but if this position is not comfortable for you, you can sit on a chair with your spine erect with make sure your back slightly away from the back

of the chair (try sitting on the front half of the seat).

- Set the timer to 5 minutes (feel free to increase the time as you become more comfortable sitting still).

- Close your eyes and begin to listen to your breath. Observe the rise and fall of your breath for a minute or two.

- Chant OM/AUM by dividing it into three parts: Aah… Oooo… Mmm…

- Repeat 3 or more times, then sit in silence while experiencing how you feel.

  o You may notice that you are salivating more (this is a normal occurrence when the Parasympathetic Nervous System is activated). You may even experience certain tingling in your face, hands, and different parts of the body which is a result from your prana – energy life force – moving and circulating around (which is a very good thing).

JOURNALING PROMPTS:

1. What did you experience during your time of Mantra practice?

2. Were you able to chant/recite the sound without feeling uneasy, silly or even critical of yourself?

3. If you did feel any of those emotions, why do you think you felt that way?

Pranayama Practice

Pranayama is Sanskrit for Breath Control. *Prana* is energy, and *Ayama* is to control. Pranayama practice plays a supporting role in getting the practitioner warmed-up for meditation on a cellular level.

Ujjayi Pranayama is also known as "Victorious Breath" or "Ocean Breath," and it is an excellent way to practice diaphragmatic breathing.

Ujjayi Pranayama

- Sit in a comfortable position with your spine in neutral position. Keep your shoulders relaxed and face soft (avoid frowning or clenching your teeth).

- Close your eyes and begin to breathe in and out through the nose, allowing the belly to expand at inhale and gently return at exhale.

- Slightly constrict your air passage in your throat and lower your chin down a little. Now start inhaling and exhaling the breath toward the back of your throat; imagine that you're taking your breath and directing it toward the inner back wall of your throat.

- It is not necessary to make your breaths noisy; keeping the breath noiseless allows the body to reduce unnecessary prana exertion.

26

JOURNALING PROMPTS:

1. What did you experience during your time of Pranayama practice?

2. Do you notice a difference between how you felt (physically, mentally, emotionally, and spiritually) before your pranayama practice vs. after your pranayama practice?

3. Write down any spiritual insights you may have received from God, and find scriptures that confirm these insights.

CHAPTER 3:
The Student Becomes the Teacher Becomes the Student

Just like many Yoga Teachers, I transitioned from the Corporate world to teaching Yoga. For over a decade, I had a successful career in the Mortgage Industry as a Business Analyst, Project Manager, and a Senior Technical Writer. I worked for several Fortune 100 Companies in California and in Texas. I successfully implemented processes and products, and I wrote corporate policies and procedures for some of the biggest financial institutions in the country. I was an ambitious, assertive, Type A corporate employee. I confidently demanded promotions and raises, which I received on a regular basis. But behind my financial and career successes, I was suffering from being overworked and chronically fatigued.

I was damaging my body and my mind by not allowing it to slow down and rest. I operated on my Sympathetic Nervous System being on high-alert at all times. I once kept myself "sharp-minded" by drinking a gigantic espresso drink and 1-2 energy drinks per day for 3 months! Thank God for His grace and mercy of protecting me from a heart attack!

The activities that I participated in fed my stress level: I took Mixed Martial Arts classes 3 times a week and Hot Yoga classes 5 times a week. These are not necessarily bad activities, but for where I was at in my life -- Type A, Driven, Ambitious, etc. -- these activities fueled my inner fire (known in Yoga & Ayurveda as *Pitta*), causing me to become easily agitated, impatient, and constantly angry.

God saved me from physical death through my family. Shawn and I had been praying about the possibility of homeschooling Jade when she started Kindergarten. I prayed specifically that if this was God's will, He would make it obvious by allowing the following things to happen prior to making the decision to homeschool:

1. We would be able to become a one-income family without any financial difficulty.

2. Jade would want to be homeschooled.

3. I would have my dream job making the most money that I had ever made and that it would hurt to resign (to make sure I wouldn't use homeschooling as an excuse to leave a job that I didn't enjoy).

Being that I've been homeschooling Jade since the beginning of the 2nd grade, you can guess what God did!

We were able to transition to becoming a one-income family without major financial strains, Jade was practically begging to be homeschooled by the middle of her 1st grade year in public school, and I resigned from my dream job as a Senior Technical Writer for a big mortgage company where I was getting paid the highest salary that I had ever made.

When I resigned, my boss' boss (whom I liked and respected greatly) tried to convince me to stay by offering me a pay-increase and the option to work from home. I remember being really tempted, but I knew that I would not be able to focus on homeschooling Jade if I accepted this offer. So as much as it hurt to turn down the offer, I did. Thus, my third request to God was answered.

Homeschooling Jade was definitely in the path that God chose for us as a family as well as for me personally: If I didn't decide to homeschool Jade, I would not have gone back into the fitness industry and then eventually pursue getting certified as a Yoga Teacher because I would not have had the time or the energy to do so after working 40+ hours per week.

I was nervous about enrolling in a 200-Hour Yoga Teacher Training. I had concerns and fears about whether or not it would cause me to struggle in my faith due to the non-Christian aspects in the eastern philosophy of yoga and what I thought a 200-Hour Yoga Teacher Training would be like. After much prayer, I decided to enroll in a program in Dallas, TX, with the intent of dropping out the minute I felt like it was negatively affecting my walk with God.

On the first day of training, my teacher (who did not specify her religious beliefs) said, "If your yoga practice does not bring you closer to God, you need to find a different style of practice." This felt like the confirmation that I needed to stay in her yoga teacher training. To this day, I repeat this quote to all of my students on the first day of my own Yoga Teacher Training program.

One of the greatest things I learned from my Yoga Teacher was that we must always be the student even when we're the teacher. The minute we stop being a student, we stop being a great teacher. When we stop having a learner's heart, we stop growing. How true this is in our everyday lives! Having a learner's heart allows us to approach each situation with humility.

I took a year off from teaching my own 200-Hour Yoga Teacher Training (YTT) so that I can focus on writing and finishing this book; but in the years that I teach my YTT program, I get to spend 13 Saturdays and 13 Sunday afternoons with the same group of people for 8-9 months. I teach them human anatomy, the subtle energy systems (including meditation and breathing techniques), yoga philosophy & history, yoga business and teaching skills.

My greatest objective in teaching my YTT program is for each of them to go through a self-transformation. Teaching them how to be a yoga teacher is secondary because, again, if they're not going through a transformation, they will not be able to help others transform through Yoga. During this process, I learn so much from them as well. I learn about my tendencies through my interaction with so many different personalities and temperaments. I learn about my teaching style as I help my students navigate through finding their own teaching styles. But the thing I love the most about learning from my students is the humility that is required to admit my shortcomings and that I am not the greatest expert at Yoga or anything else for that matter. It is at the center of humility that you will find the atman. (See Figure 1.3 on page 14.)

Whenever I go through phases of arrogance – whether intentionally or unintentionally – I find myself taking God out of the equation. It becomes all about ME. There is a difference between drawing inward for introspection (in meditation) and becoming self-focused.

One of my favorite Christian authors is Francis Chan. In his book, *Crazy Love: Overwhelmed by a Relentless God* [2], he compares life to a movie. He mentions that God is the main character. The movie is about Him, and we're the supporting cast in His movie. When I start to believe that I'm the main character of this movie called LIFE, I stop learning and realizing that it's not about me! Learning, to a degree, is an outward-focused action; Even when we start to apply what we learn, we're not changing the learned information to mirror our lives; we're changing our perspectives/beliefs/convictions to mirror the learned information.

I make it a point to read a lot of books to help keep me on this path of learning. The topics that I mostly read about are yoga, Ayurveda, meditation, human anatomy, self-help books, Christianity/Discipleship, and neuroscience. I also take workshops and classes from well-respected and reputable Yoga Teachers and Christian Teachers/Speakers. Some of my favorites are Nikki Myers, Rod Stryker, Guy Hammond, and Gordon Ferguson.

[2] *Chan, F. (2008). Crazy Love: Overwhelmed by a Relentless God, pp.44-46.*

In addition to books, classes and workshops, I love learning from people in all walks of life. Shawn (my husband) and I help lead the teen ministry at church, and I learn so much from the teen guys and girls. I learn from their struggles, their victories, and their desire to put God first even though they are bombarded on a daily basis with giving into peer pressure, pleasure-seeking, mediocrity, bullying, and walking away from their authenticity. I have so much respect for these young adults.

If you're an adult, I invite you to spend some judgment-free time with a teenager. If you're a teenager, I invite you to spend some judgement-free time with an adult. When you approach time with others without judgement, you will be amazed at how much you're able to learn and grow.

Be the student. Be the teacher. And then be the student again.

TECHNIQUE:

Pranayama and Mantra Practice

"So-Hum" (the natural sound of the breath)

In this mantra practice, you will chant internally where your intention becomes the voice of the spirit.

- Set the timer for 3 minutes.

- Sit tall, either on the floor using a pillow/meditation cushion, or on a chair with your feet flat on the floor hip-width apart and your spine in neutral. Make sure you're not leaning on the back of the chair.

- Close your eyes and begin to breathe through the nose, effortlessly and noiselessly. Notice the rise and fall of the belly as you inhale and exhale.

- Notice the silent sound of the breath. As you breathe, you may intuitively hear the sound "So" at inhale and the sound "Hum." Do this until your timer goes off.

- Sit still for a minute and just observe how you feel.

JOURNALING PROMPTS:

1. What did you experience during your time of Pranayama-Mantra practice?

2. Were you able to chant silently without feeling uneasy, silly or even critical of yourself?

3. If you did feel any of those emotions, why do you think
    you felt that way?

Bhramari Pranayama

"Bhramari" comes from the word bhramar which is Sanskrit for bee. This breathing exercise gets its name from the buzzing sound that is made during the exhalation.

Bhramari Pranayama is known to soothe nerves and balance one's energy.

- Set the timer to 3 minutes.

- Sit tall, either on the floor using a pillow/meditation cushion, or on a chair with your feet flat on the floor hip-width apart and making sure you're not leaning on the back of the chair. Make sure your spine is in neutral position.

- Using the tip of index fingers, plug your ears. (Alternatively, you can use ear plugs so that you can rest your hands on your lap.)

- Close your throat slightly (like Ujjayi pranayama) so that you can gently hear your inhales and exhales.

- Close your eyes and take a deep inhale through the nose, and allow the sound MMM to take place as you exhale.

- Repeat until the timer goes off.

JOURNALING PROMPTS:

1. What did you experience during your time of Pranayama practice?

2. How did you feel (physically, mentally, emotionally, and spiritually) before your pranayama practice vs. after your pranayama practice?

3. Write down any spiritual insights you may have received from God, and find scriptures that confirm these insights.

Drishti Meditation

- Set the timer to 5 minutes.

- Find a small item that you want to focus on. It could be a candle, a cross, or anything that you can focus on.

- Breathe effortlessly and noiselessly as you focus on the object.

- Continue to breathe as you relax your eyes and allow your gaze to go past the object as if you're looking through it.

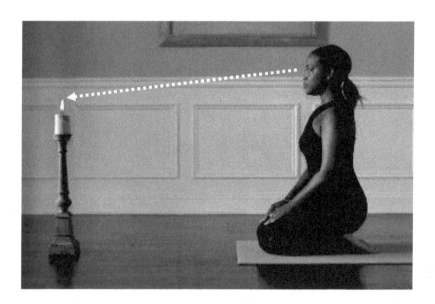

JOURNALING PROMPTS:

1. Were you able to focus for the entire 5 minutes? If not, what prevented you from focusing for the entire 5 minutes?

2. Write down any thoughts or feelings that may have surfaced during your meditation practice.

3. Write down any spiritual insights you may have received from God, and find scriptures that confirm these insights.

CHAPTER 4:
Journey to the Atman

I have a confession to make; I don't meditate every day. I try to meditate every day, but once in a while, I have days when my spiritual near-sightedness wants to bypass this much needed time because "my schedule is way too packed!" Even as I say this, I can't help but laugh at the irony in this thought process! It's when I'm "too busy" that I need to meditate more than ever! Without meditation, my prayer times with God becomes shallow. Without incorporating this "Be still and know that I am God" moments, I try to become of the lord of my own life.

On the days that I don't meditate, I find myself reverting to my sinful nature (Romans 7:21-25). When I'm not spending times in meditation with God, I find myself struggling more with these things:

1. Insecurity (especially about my physical appearance and my authenticity.)

2. Selfishness (I don't want to be inconvenienced.)

3. Short-temperedness (I get irritated with minor things.)

4. Manipulation/Selfish Ambition (I try to control the outcome of situations for my own benefit.)

5. Pride (Everything becomes a competition.)

6. Apathetic (I don't connect with people's pains because that takes "too much effort.")

7. Uncaring (I become numb to people's pains and discomforts.)

8. Violent (I could feel my blood "boil" when I get upset.)

On the contrary, this is how I am when I take the time out to meditate and become clothed with Him (Christ):

1. Secure (I am perfect in His sight, and I can be spiritually authentic. Psalm 139:13-14)

2. Selfless (I want to meet needs of those around me. Philippians 2:3-4)

3. Patient (Because God is patient with me so that I can repent. 2 Peter 3:9)

4. At Peace (I'm surrendered to God's will. Philippians 4:7)

5. Humble (Saying this sounds prideful, but what I mean is that it's much easier to imitate Jesus' humility. Philippians 2:1-4)

6. Empathetic (My heart breaks for people who are hurting, and I trust God by breaking down the walls of selfishness. Romans 12:15)

7. Caring (I want to help carry people's burdens. Galatians 6:2)

8. Merciful (I choose to let things go and in clear conscience, let God be the judge. Matthew 5:7)

The fact that the second list is within my reach, it makes more sense for me to take some time to meditate and experience an invaluable intimacy with Him!

TECHNIQUE:

Pranayama Practice

Viloma

In Sanskrit, Vi means "against", and Loma means "hair." Combined, Viloma means "against the hair" or "against the natural order of things."

1. Viloma on the Inhale

   - Set the timer to 3 minutes.

   - Close your eyes and place your hands on your lap or knees, palms up.

   - Take a few slow, deep 1:1 breaths.

   - Now divide your inhales into three parts with a quick pause in between, and exhale the same count.

     o For example, if you're inhaling and exhaling for 6 counts: Inhale for 2 counts, pause, inhale for 2 counts, pause, inhale for 2 counts, pause, exhale for 6 counts, pause.

   - Repeat until the timer goes off.

2. Viloma on the Exhale

   - Set the timer to 3 minutes.

   - Close your eyes and place your hands on your lap or knees, palms down.

- Take a few slow, deep 1:1 breaths.

- Now Inhale, then divide your exhales into three parts with a quick pause in between.

  - For example, if you're inhaling and exhaling for 6 counts: Inhale for 6 counts, pause, exhale for 2 counts, pause, exhale for 2 counts, pause, exhale for 2 counts, pause.

- Repeat until the timer goes off.

3. Viloma on the Inhale and Exhale

- Set the timer to 3 minutes.

- Close your eyes and place your hands on your lap or knees, palms up or down.

- Take a few slow, deep 1:1 breaths.

- Now divide your inhales and exhales into three parts with a quick pause in between.

  - For example, if you're inhaling and exhaling for 6 counts: Inhale for 2 counts, pause, inhale for 2 counts, pause, inhale for 2 counts, pause, exhale for 2 counts, pause, exhale for 2 counts, pause, exhale for 2 counts, pause.

- Repeat until the timer goes off.

JOURNALING PROMPTS:

1. Were you able to stay still the entire time during the pranayama practice? If not, what prevented you from focusing for the entire 5 minutes?

2. Out of the three Viloma Pranayama practices, which one did you like the most? Why?

Color Meditation

In this 30-minute meditation, I will guide you through a practice where you will utilize your ability to visualize colors along with a pranayama practice. The recording can be downloaded by going to my website, under the "Resources" tab (password protected):

https://www.jhenisolis.com/resources/colormeditation

(Password: **Psalm4610**)

JOURNALING PROMPTS:

1. Write down any thoughts or feelings that may have surfaced during your Color Meditation practice.

2. Write down any spiritual insights you may have received from God, and find scriptures that confirm these insights.

CHAPTER 5:
Molehills and Mountains

Throughout our lives, we experience many challenges and situations that make us want to crawl into a hole and never come out. The following stories come from the lives of several people (including my own) and the healing which took place through stillness in biblical meditation. To protect their privacy, all of the names – other than mine – have been changed.

Part 1: Daily Stressors

I have the privilege of teaching classes, certification workshops and continuing education workshops to many individuals in the yoga, wellness and fitness industries in several states. I love meeting new people and getting to know them in the short time we share together. One of my most favorite things is to watch my students go through transformations and get closer to their spiritual centers.

One of the first things Stella mentioned to me when we met was that she wasn't sure if she should be attending my workshop. She felt that maybe she was too new to Yoga to take such an in-depth workshop. I reassured her that she was meant to be there and that because she is fairly new to Yoga, she was coming in with a clean slate and with no preconceived notions or history of bad habits (like my years of improper alignment that I mentioned in Chapter 2 of this book). As she attended almost all of my workshops that year, we got to know each other better and have some great talks about God, our Christian faiths, life, and everything in between.

About two years before attending one of my workshops, Stella was feeling like her life had become stagnant and each day felt repetitive. She had been working for the same company for 20 years where she experienced many successes professionally. She felt blessed to have been able to make such a great impact within the workplace, but her dedication to the company left very little time for her personal life.

Stella found herself constantly wondering why she felt like something was missing. Her marriage was great, and she had more than enough friends and family to fill up her limited social schedule. She and her husband Michael started eating healthier, exercising regularly, and she began to take yoga classes. They were active members of their church. Even with all these "blessings," Stella felt like something was missing and couldn't understand why she would often feel irritated with people.

As she began to dig deeper, Stella started to question everything she was doing and all the relationships she had in her life. She examined her heart and asked herself these questions in regards to her commitments: "How much of it is really enhancing my life," "How much of it is bringing me joy," and "How much of it is because I feel obligated in some way to do it?" After this self-inquiry, she realized that the source of her irritation and impatience with people came from feeling obligated to do things out of wanting to please people.

She knew she was happy about:

- Her relationship with God (She knew that He is the SOURCE and everything else is just a RESOURCE.)

- Her marriage (Michael was, without a doubt, her best friend.)

- Yoga (She loved it. Period.)

She knew she was not happy about:

- Her over-commitment at church – She was serving in five different programs at church, but in reality, she knew she was only passionate about two of those programs.

- Unhealthy relationships – Certain friends and family members would use her as a dumping ground for their problems and gossip which left her feeling hurt and taken advantage of.

- Having no children due to fertility issues – She and Michael had always felt surrendered to God about this matter, but for some reason, she was now questioning her worth as a woman.

Even after making her analysis, she still struggled with self-pity, resentment and distrust. She continued to pray to God for guidance and clarity.

One day while she was at church, the minister asked everyone to close their eyes and meditate for about 3 minutes. This was a familiar territory for Stella, since she already experienced short meditations in yoga classes. Meditation wasn't something she took all that seriously in the past, but she decided to take the minister's challenge of meditating every day for a week before starting her morning routine. As she sat in stillness and focused on her scripture readings, she began to experience a transformation of her heart. Incorporating biblical meditation in her home yoga practice allowed her to experience more clarity from God about her life.

Stella found that she didn't feel as stressed about life and the unimportant things seemed to matter less and less. She felt clearer and stronger about her decisions as she established some healthy boundaries with others. One of the scriptures that carried her through much of her resentment towards people was Romans 8:26-32:

"In the same way, the Spirit helps us in our weakness. We do not know what we ought to pray for, but the Spirit himself intercedes for us through wordless groans.

And he who searches our hearts knows the mind of the Spirit, because the Spirit intercedes for God's people in accordance with the will of God.

And we know that in all things God works for the good of those who love him, who have been called according to his purpose. For those God foreknew he also predestined to be conformed to the image of his Son, that he might be the firstborn among many brothers and sisters. And those he predestined, he also called; those he called, he also justified; those he justified, he also glorified.

What, then, shall we say in response to these things? If God is for us, who can be against us? He who did not spare his own Son, but gave him up for us all—how will he not also, along with him, graciously give us all things?"

These scriptures spoke to Stella because she wasn't sure what she was really seeking God for or how to put her feelings and thoughts into words – so she felt the need for God to intercede on her behalf. She recited over and over again the reminder, "If God is for us, who can be against us?"

As she stood firm on her new-found boundaries, Stella experienced the loss of few friendships that could not accept that she was no longer a dumping ground for their gossip and negative speech. Thankfully, the family members that once took her for granted began to slowly change for the better. Whereas in the past similar conflicts with people would have caused her to crawl under a rock, she now has peace and more fulfillment in surrounding herself with people that are mutually encouraging and aimed at glorifying God.

Her new conviction on her boundaries has helped in the workplace as well. In the past, she would work 11-hour days without hesitation; After communicating with her boss and colleagues of her new work hours (which totaled 8 hours per day), she experienced a shift in the departmental culture as more and more people began adopting this policy. Nowadays, it is understood that Stella will not accept any meeting invitations scheduled to end less than 30 minutes before for "clock-out" time. Her work productivity has not decreased, and she has learned that working as if she was working for the Lord for 8 hours each workday was more than enough for her to finish everything that she needed to.

Meditating has additionally helped Stella in understand that being childless transforms the way she sees God working through her. She recognizes that being the woman God has called her to be should be her only desire. Isaiah 55:8 reads, "For my thoughts, are not your thoughts, neither are your ways, my ways." Meditation on this reminds her that she really doesn't really know what is right and fair, because only God knows. She has discovered that she, alone, are more than enough and that the stillness she experiences in meditation keeps her closer to Him.

Through experiencing stillness in her biblical meditation practice, she came to realize that the main source of her stress came from lack of boundaries; and through this realization, she was finally able to release her tight grip on stress.

Part 2: Childhood Trauma

Ann was 31 years old when she began having memories of being abused as a child. As she was driving home after picking her daughter up from a friend's house, she was hit with a flashback of when she was abused by her babysitter at age 7. She and her family had temporarily moved in with her cousins, and she was placed in the care of a neighbor after school for a couple of times per week.

The babysitter, Nicole, was in her mid-20's, and she seemed more like a big sister to Ann and to the two other kids that she watched. One day when Ann was sitting down with the other kids having a snack, Nicole came over and sat with them. Without any hesitation, the other kids began to touch Nicole inappropriately while she sat back and closed her eyes. Ann shifted in her seat uncomfortably, not knowing what to do. She had never had a babysitter before, so she thought that maybe this was supposed to be normal. After being pressured by the other kids to join in, Ann reluctantly gave in.

This continued for several weeks until she and her family moved to a more permanent residence about an hour away. She never told her parents out of shame, but her behaviors began to change. She started to gravitate towards male friendships and constantly questioned the motives of the few female friends she had. She began to view all physical touch as sexual advances, so she avoided classmates who were physically affectionate. As a teen, she craved affection and attention from guys. By the time she was in college, she was sleeping around, drinking heavily, and smoking constantly. She also struggled with eating disorders all throughout her teen years.

When Ann began to have these flashbacks, she became angry at God. She cried out to God many nights asking why He would reveal her abuse in her 30's. She felt that she was doing just fine in her life and would've been fine not knowing this fact for the rest of her life.

Once she got over her anger, she began to question whether or not what she went through was truly abuse. As a mother, she asked herself, "If this happened to my child, would I consider it abuse?" The answer was a resounding YES!

She decided to start the healing process through techniques she learned through professional counseling and through meditation. The meditation technique I recommended to her was to practice being still for 5 minutes while focusing on her breath followed by a guided meditation. While in stillness, God revealed the following things to her:

1. It was not her fault.

2. She was not ready to know about the abuse sooner than it was revealed to her because she would not have been able to handle it and heal from it in a godly way.

3. Hurt people hurt people.

She also realized that this has caused her to struggle with being vulnerable in her relationships. She was always very open and spoke of her life and struggles in a very matter-of-fact way with very little emotions attached.

She was able to heal the first layer of the trauma. What I mean by first layer is this: We are complex beings, with many layers to who we are. In Yoga, this is called *Koshas* (See Figure 1.3 on page 14).

Just like an onion, we discover deeper layers to who we are as we peel away each layer. And just like an onion, each layer that we peel away can cause us to shed some tears. But it is through peeling away the layers that we're able to reach the Atman.

If you have experienced sexual abuse, I strongly advise you to seek professional help. You can find resources through National Sexual Violence Resource Center at www.nsvrc.org.

Part 3: Marital Hardships and Transitions

Sheryl is a happily married, mother of three kids. She and her husband Tom are known for their hospitality, generosity, and compassion among many other great things. She is joyful, patient, and content. But it took her over two decades to get to that point.

Sheryl had been a Christian for 5 years when she met Justin at church. They had a whirlwind dating relationship and got married a few months after. Throughout their short dating relationship, it was very clear that her focus was on getting married. There were some red flags of his controlling nature before their marriage, but she was naïve and chose to ignore the alarming signs that they were not focused on God.

She recounts a time when she actually broke up with him. After ending things with Justin near his home, she got in her car to make the hour-long drive back to her house. About half way into her drive, she looked in the rearview mirror and saw that Justin had been following her! As they both pulled over, he proceeded to cry and beg for her to take him back and that he could not live without her. She compromised on her initial decision and got back together with him.

After they got married, Justin's controlling behavior escalated quickly from anger to violence. Sheryl's first memory of his violent behavior was during their honeymoon when he threw a coffee cup across the room during an argument. Shortly after that incident, he began hitting her and displaying terrifying behaviors. Within their first year in marriage, she became depressed and emotionally detached from the world.

After being reached out to by a concerned co-worker, she got down on her knees in prayer and began to evaluate where she had been spiritually the past several years. As she began to make changes in her spiritual focus, she sought out counseling. By the end of their first year in marriage, she made the decision to leave Justin. They decided to get help separately; him, in anger management and her, in therapy.

Things began to improve between them, and they decided to get back together. Although Justin was no longer hitting her, Sheryl knew that the underlying issues in their marriage still remained. They moved half was across the country to get a fresh start.

Quickly after their move, she became pregnant. Things between Sheryl and Justin continued to be up and down in the typical and a cyclical manner of an abusive relationship.

Things got dramatically worse after their second child was born. Justin became very bitter and dissatisfied with life, and he stopped trying to overcome his anger issues. Sheryl's hopes and dreams for a better marriage were shattered as she went into survival mode. In her hopelessness, she asked herself, "Is this going to be my life? Am I going to be 50 years-old one day and feel completely beaten down?" Things had to get worse before they can become better.

They were on a family trip to visit family when they got lost. His frustrations turned into anger, which quickly turned into rage and violence. He started punching her in the car as he yelled, "I'm gonna kill you and leave you in the woods!" Their young daughters were in the backseat, completely terrified. The entire time, she prayed and begged for God to save her.

After this incident, her health began to decline. She feared that if she opened up to her friends, Justin would somehow hear her conversations. It was during this darkest of dark time that she threw herself to God and begged for complete surrender to Him and a peace that only comes from Him. Through her quiet stillness and through her loud cries for mercy, God showed her that she did everything she possibly could and that she had options for a better life. After almost 9 years of marriage, Sheryl left Justin for good and took the children with her. She got herself a lawyer and did whatever she needed to do to get back on her feet.

Even with financial challenges as a single mom, she felt like a bird that had been set free. She was able to get a great job which led to a better job, which led to even a better job. She felt blessed beyond words.

About 5 years into her single motherhood, she became aware of a man that caught her heart. She noticed his heart for God, his gentleness, kindness, humility and complete transparency about his life. By this time though, Sheryl was a different person. She did not want to take a step to the right or to the left without God's approval. She prayed that God would make it clear if Tom was the one by allowing him to fall in love with her... because she knew she was already in love with him.

Dating and marrying Tom was like a fairytale for Sheryl. She felt like Cinderella who met her Prince Charming. Their marriage was filled with bliss even through the challenges of many court appearances regarding the two children she shared with Justin.

Sheryl has recently celebrated her 50th Birthday which she describes as an incredibly glorious moment. She is finally able to answer the question that her 30-year-old self once had; "No, you will not at 50 years old feel completely beaten down. Your life will be better than you can ever imagine!" She now feels surrendered. She sees this as a time for herself to grab ahold of thoughts and feelings as she strives to be unwavering in her joy in Christ.

When she looks back to her past, she can hardly recognize her old self. She can reflect to those days of devastating challenges and smile because she has no bitterness towards her ex-husband. She believes that because forgiveness was what was given to her by God, she needs to give forgiveness to others. She is certain that somehow, someway, everything she experienced was all part of God's plan.

She uses the scriptures to ponder and meditate on throughout the day. When she struggles with having faith, she fights in her heart until she becomes faithful. She does this by sitting in stillness as she contemplates over scriptures. Some of the scriptures that she uses during her times of stillness and meditation are Romans 5:3-5 and Romans 12:12. She pushes off her thoughts and allows the scriptures to take over her heart. She also recites scriptures throughout the day, holding God to His promises. Sheryl has made God her ultimate counselor as she pours over his Word.

For assistance in Domestic Violence, please go to the website for National Resource Center on Domestic Violence at https://nrcdv.org.

Part 4: Addictions

In March of this year (2019), I went through a 3-day training for a program called Y12SR™, which stands for Yoga of 12-Step Recovery. I expected the weekend to be about incorporating yoga into an already-existing 12-step recovery program, but it turned out to be so much more than that. The teacher talked about not only chemical addictions but also co-dependency which can be best described as, "anything that you use outside of yourself for satisfaction, pleasure, or fulfillment." So, in essence, we're all co-dependent!

Co-dependency causes us to be fixated on the object of our addiction (person, environment, substance, etc.). Our thoughts become consumed with anything and everything that relates to it. We become so blinded by the pleasure and security we experience, that it's nearly impossible to see how destructive it really is.

In 1948, Albert Einstein wrote a letter to his friend, psychiatrist Otto Julius Burger. In it, he wrote, "I believe that the abominable deterioration of ethical standards stems primarily from the mechanization and depersonalization of our lives, a disastrous byproduct of science and technology. Nostra culpa[2]!" This has since been paraphrased as, "I fear the day that technology will surpass our human interaction. The world will have a generation of idiots." These prophetic words are so applicable today.

As I write these words, I'm sitting at a Panera Bread in Charlotte, NC, and I see a man on his cell phone, four people on their laptops, and a handful of people on their smart phones. When I go to the gym, I see people taking selfies of their workouts.

When I go to Starbucks, I see majority of the customers sipping their drinks while fully fixated on their phones. I'm also guilty of this, as on the days that I unintentionally leave my phone at home, I go about the rest of the day feeling like a huge part of me is missing. This addiction we have to technology is just as dangerous to our spirituality as any other addictions.

[2] *Nostra Culpa – Latin for "Our Fault"*

So, what do we do about these addictions and co-dependencies?

1. We must recognize that we have an addiction.

2. We must take ownership of our shortcomings and admit that we are powerless without the help of a higher power (God) (Psalm 32:5).

3. We must become transparent of our wrongdoings (sins) to God and to others so that we can begin to repent and heal from the wounds that our bad decisions have caused (James 5:16).

4. We must make a commitment to live differently and make moment by moment decisions that are less about us and more about the One that's greater than us.

> When we confess and become transparent with others, I encourage you to use wisdom in who you confess and share your sins. It is best to get open with people that can help you through prayer, encouragement, challenge and accountability.

"He must become greater; I must become less."

John 3:30

Part 5: Mourning the Death of a Loved One

My dad and I had always been close. Even when I was going through my "rebellious teenager" stage, I knew I was going to be okay because my dad was the pillar that I could always lean on; so when he was diagnosed with Stage 4B Lung Cancer, I felt like the ground had given out underneath me.

Shawn and I had been married for 2 years when my dad started having difficulty breathing. He went to a clinic and had some fluids drained from his lungs, and we all hoped that it was pneumonia. After the fluids were sent to the lab, he received a call to make an appointment for more tests. My family and I were all in denial that it could be cancer (even though my dad had smoked all of his adult life and had been around carcinogenic chemicals when my parents owned a dry cleaners). I will never forget the day my dad and I sat with the doctor who gave us the diagnosis, "You are in the advanced stage of lung cancer."

My dad went through a little over 1 ½ years of treatments including chemotherapy before he passed away on August 23, 2005. I went into an automatic-pilot mode as I watched my dad take his last breaths and as I held my mom who was sobbing into my arms. I had to continue keeping my composure through making all the calls to my brother, uncles and aunts. Thankfully, my brother and my uncles took care of all the funeral arrangements. I felt numb throughout the funeral, and I didn't fall apart until a few days after.

I woke up 2 days after the funeral with extreme pain in my entire right side. My hip felt buckled, and I couldn't move without experiencing jolting pain shoot through my spine. I made an appointment with an acupuncturist in my neighborhood for the next day.

During my acupuncture session, she placed needles on my right side, from the top of my head all the way down to my toes. Lying on my left side hugging a body pillow, I began to weep. I was confused and embarrassed for crying uncontrollably. When I tried to stop, the acupuncturist said, "Just let the tears flow. This is your body's way of releasing the sadness that's been trapped inside. You must allow yourself to have this emotional release in order to heal." (This took me back to my first real savasana experience.) After one more acupuncture session with her, I was able to move freely without any pain.

When we don't acknowledge our emotions as they happen, they become stagnant in our bodies. Through my training in energy science, I have learned that emotions travel straight to the heart first. If they don't get filtered out and resolved, they travel down to the hips. The right side of our bodies hold the "solar" energy, which represents the more masculine aspects of who we are (including the male figures in our lives). Consequently, the left side of our bodies hold the "lunar" energy, which represents the feminine aspects of who we are (including the female figures in our lives). Having learned this, it makes sense that my right side became buckled and I felt the pain mostly in my right hip (since I stuffed my grief and sadness immediately after my dad died).

The more we allow the Holy Spirit to flow freely in our bodies without the emotional molehills and mountains we create, the closer we will get to experiencing stillness and inner peace.

Once the emotional and spiritual blockages of grief were lifted, I was able to begin my mourning process. The statement, "Take one step at a time" never rang truer than those days, weeks and months. I had never felt such a myriad of intense emotions in my entire life: I felt regret for having Jade (she was 9 months old when my dad died) because the thought of her one day having to go through losing me and/or Shawn was beyond devastating. I felt angry at my dad for smoking for 40+ years, for abandoning us and for making my mom a widow. I felt relieved that my mom, brother and I no longer had to take turns taking care of him and being constantly exhausted from taking him to all the appointments, meeting with the case workers, etc. I felt guilty for feeling relieved. I felt grateful that God allowed me to have a wonderful earthly dad for 31 years, knowing full well that not everyone has a great dad. For about a year after his death these are the emotions that would overtake me… until one night when he was in my dream.

In my dream, I called my mom. The phone rang twice, and then I heard a voice on the other line. "Hello?" he asked. I immediately recognized my dad's voice. The rest of the phone call went something like this:

Me: "Dad? What are you doing answering the phone? You know you died, right?"

My dad: "Yeah, I know, (chuckles) I just like messing with your mom and playing pranks on people. I couldn't help it."

Me: "Dad, you can't be doing things like that! It'll freak people out!"

My dad: "Haha, I know... Okay, I'll stop. Here's your mom."

My mom: "Hello?"

Me: "Mom... He's doing it again. He's answering the phone."

My mom: "I know. I keep telling him to stop, but you know how your dad is. Always trying to get a good laugh!"

I started to heal and have more good days than bad after that dream.

I don't think we ever fully heal from losing a loved one. I think when our hearts experience such a deep loss, that emotional wound becomes a scar, and that scar triggers moments of sadness for the rest of our lives; but I have come to accept this because I see it is a reminder of how much I love him.

If you are experiencing a difficult time coping with grief from loss of loved ones, please reach out for support and/or contact a mental health professional near you.

TECHNIQUE:

Mudra and Pranayama Practice

Anjali Mudra and 1:2 Breath Pranayama

In this mudra and pranayama practice, the goal is to become a participant in the observation of your spirit.

- Set the timer for 5 minutes.

- Sit tall, either on the floor using a pillow/meditation cushion, or on a chair with your feet flat on the floor hip-width apart while making sure you don't lean on the back of the chair. Bring your spine in a neutral position.

- Close your eyes and bring your palms together at heart-center (like a prayer pose).

- Begin to breathe through the nose, effortlessly and noiselessly. Notice the rise and fall of the belly as you inhale and exhale.

- Begin 1:2 Breath Pranayama

  o Inhale for 4 counts, then exhale for 4 counts.

- with each breath, lengthen the exhales until you reach an inhale of 4 counts and exhale of 8 counts. Continue this 1:2 breathing.

- Experience listening to the silent sound of the breath as you internally repeat, (Inhale) "He must become greater," (Exhale) "I must become less." Do not analyze the scripture. Just experience the stillness. Do this until the timer goes off.

- Sit still for a minute and just observe how you feel.

JOURNALING PROMPTS:

1. What did you experience during your time of Mudra and Pranayama practice?

2. Were you able to sit still silently without feeling uneasy, silly or even critical of yourself?

3. If you did feel any of those emotions, why do you think you felt that way?

4. How did you feel (physically, mentally, emotionally, and spiritually) before your mudra and pranayama practice vs. after your mudra and pranayama practice?

5. Write down any spiritual insights you may have received from God in regards to Him becoming greater and you becoming less, and find scriptures that confirm these insights.

Pranayama Practice

Nadi Shodhana (Alternate Nostril Breathing)

- Face the right palm towards your face and bend the index and middle fingers down:

- Set the timer to 3 minutes.

- Using the tip of your ring finger, plug your left nostril as you inhale through the right nostril.

- Unplug your left nostril and plug your right nostril with your thumb as you exhale AND inhale through the left nostril.

- Unplug your right nostril as you plug your left nostril while you exhale.

- Repeat until the timer goes off.

JOURNALING PROMPTS:

1. What did you experience during your pranayama practice?

2. How would you be able to incorporate Savasana for physical, mental, emotional, and spiritual benefits?

3. Write down any spiritual insights you may have received from God, and find scriptures that confirm these insights.

Yoga Nidra

Yoga Nidra is translated as "Yogic Sleep." It's like a guided relaxation journey. In savasana, you listen to the guide (usually a yoga or a meditation teacher) as they take you through a visualization of various things and scenarios.

Some of the benefits of Yoga Nidra are:

- Mental Balance

- Emotional Balance

- Increase in Serotonin (the "happy" neurotransmitters)

- Increase in Memory

- Increase in Concentration

- Reduction in Stress

- Reduction in Anxiety and Depression

- Improvement in the quality of sleep

What happens to the brain during Yoga Nidra?

Yoga Nidra slows down the brainwaves to enter a state of balance mentally and emotionally while promoting mindfulness.

During Yoga Nidra, the eta brain waves decrease (promoting healing on a cellular level), and the Alpha, Theta and delta brain waves increase (producing a rise in serotonin levels – the "feel good" hormones – as well as strengthening the immune system and regenerates the nerve cells).

In addition to this, 30 minutes of Yoga Nidra is equivalent to 2-4 hours of sleep!

I don't suggest that you replace sleep with Yoga Nidra, but it is a great practice for when you feel sleep-deprived or mentally tired as well as any other time you need some relaxation, mental rest, or a deep journey within your soul.

To access the password-protected recording for the Yoga Nidra practice, go to:
https://www.jhenisolis.com/resources/yoganidra
(Password: **Psalm4610**)

JOURNALING PROMPTS:

1. What did you experience during your time of Yoga Nidra practice?

2. Were you able to lie still and follow the guidance? If not, what was the obstacle? (A wandering mind? Physically uncomfortable?)

3. How did you feel (physically, mentally, emotionally, and spiritually) before your Yoga Nidra practice vs. after your Yoga Nidra practice?

4. Write down any spiritual insights you may have received about the nature of God, and find scriptures that confirm these insights.

CHAPTER 6:
Lessons from Discomfort

We're all comfort-seeking creatures. We want to be well-rested, stress-free, worry-free and pain-free. Our instincts tell us to avoid anything/anyone that we perceive to be the cause of our discomfort, but we rarely stop to dig deeper within ourselves to evaluate our perceptions.

Not all discomforts are bad. In 2015, I heard about the benefits of whole-body cryotherapy which can include relief in joint and muscle pain, speeding up the healing process of injuries, improvement in chronic pain associated with arthritis, fibromyalgia, and many more. In a typical session, you stand in a closed chamber (with your head sticking out) for about 3 minutes. During these 3 minutes, the chamber's temperature drops to approximately -275 degrees Fahrenheit.

I went twice a week for a few months in Allen, TX before moving to Charlotte. During this time, I was teaching a lot of group fitness and yoga classes as well as teaching workshops all over the North Dallas area. In addition to teaching, I was exercising 5 times a week which left me sore and achy almost every day.

Don't let the smile fool you; I was shivering and my teeth were chattering!

I found that my cryotherapy sessions reduced   soreness and gave me a burst of energy after each session; however, during those 3 minutes, I was shivering and felt extremely uncomfortable!

Even though those 3 minutes caused a lot of discomfort, the after-effect kept me coming back for more. In addition, cryotherapy helped me alleviate some of the pain I was left with after a bad whiplash I experienced from a car accident.

As someone that has been exercising since youth, I like setting fitness goals for myself. One year, I decided that my goal for that year was to be able to do 100 pushups. My starting point was 10 pushups. Every day, I worked on doing as many pushups as I can in 90 seconds as well as weight training using my dumbbells. In 4-5 months, I was able to do 100 pushups! The training process was not comfortable, but it was working through the discomfort that allowed me to achieve my goal that year.

There have been many times in my life where I was in very uncomfortable situations personally, spiritually, financially, and relationally. In my early 20's, I was desperately wanting to move out of my parents' house for independence. Keep in mind, I was living rent-free at my parents' house with no bills to pay. They didn't enforce a curfew or any strict rules. I came and went as I pleased. But in my immature, irresponsible mind, I felt that moving out to live with my friends would be a great idea. So, against my parents' advice, I moved out to share a 2-bedroom apartment with two of my friends in Tarzana, CA.

The honeymoon phase of my "adult-life" came quickly to an end when I realized that I had to now live paycheck to paycheck with very little money left over after paying for rent, bills and food. The fact that toilet paper doesn't grow on trees and a new tube of toothpaste doesn't magically appear brought me to live very uncomfortably for some time until I was able to get a higher-paying job. Although I don't recommend learning responsibility this way, the discomfort I felt allowed me to become more disciplined with my spending habits and budgeting.

You might be going through a time of discomfort right now. You might be in a situation where you feel like there's no end in sight. You may even be considering throwing in the towel and taking the "easier" way out. But before you do, ask yourself these questions:

1. Why do you want to get out of the discomfort? (Move beyond the answer of, "Because it doesn't feel good," or "Because I can.")

2. What would you accomplish if you didn't stay in discomfort?

3. What would you accomplish if you stay in discomfort?

4. Would the accomplishments of staying in discomfort outweigh the accomplishments of getting out of discomfort?

5. If getting out of discomfort has greater benefits, what do you need to do to get out of it?

Other than the discomfort resulting from poor choices, God speaks about the benefits of persevering in hard times:

- *"Be joyful in hope, patient in affliction, faithful in prayer."* (Romans 12:12)

- *"Let us not become weary in doing good, for at the proper time we will reap a harvest if we do not give up."* (Galatians 6:9)

- *"Blessed is the one who perseveres under trial because, having stood the test, that person will receive the crown of life that the Lord has promised to those who love Him."* (James 1:12)

- *"And as for you, brothers and sisters, never tire of doing what is good."* (2 Thessalonians 3:13)

- *"Watch your life and doctrine closely. Persevere in them, because if you do, you will save both yourself and your hearers."* (1 Timothy 4:16)

A Word on Stillness

Stillness can't happen when you're resisting discomfort. To resist is to put your effort and energy into defeating it. Instead of resisting or fighting it, I invite you to acknowledge the discomfort and remind yourself that the discomfort will not result in death. Maybe through this acknowledgement, you will experience the joy of surrender to stillness.

TECHNIQUE:

Stillness Meditation

In this 30-minute meditation, I will guide you through a visualization of stillness combined with a pranayama practice. The recording can be downloaded by going to my website, under the "Resources" tab (password protected):

https://www.jhenisolis.com/resources/stillnessmeditation
(Password: **Psalm4610**)

JOURNALING PROMPTS:

1. What did you experience during your time of meditation?

2. If you experienced any physical, mental or emotional discomforts during the meditation, were you able to acknowledge, accept, and surrender to stillness?

3. Write down any spiritual insights you may have received from God, and find scriptures that confirm these insights.

CHAPTER 7:
The Journey Continues

National Institute of Mental Health (NIMH) reported that 18.1 percent (approximately 40 million) of adults in the United States are affected by Anxiety Disorders and 7.1 percent (approximately 17.3 million) of adults had some form of major depressive episode. Anxiety and Depression Research Center at UCLA stated that "Anxiety is a response to danger or threat[3] and Harvard Health Publishing stated that, "there are many possible causes of depression, including faulty mood regulation by the brain, genetic vulnerability, stressful life events, medications, and medical problems[4]." Although various factors can cause anxiety and/or depression, one of the sources of both are stress.

When the body and/or the mind goes through stressful situations, the Sympathetic Nervous System (SNS) is activated for self-preservation purposes. This autonomic response is very important in life-threatening situations, but the body tends to experience the activation of SNS more often than required.

In order to combat the activation of SNS, the Parasympathetic Nervous System (PNS) must be activated. One of the most effective ways of doing this is through meditation and controlled breathing. When we breathe right, our nervous systems can begin to return to homeostasis. As our bodies relax, our minds are able to relax. When our minds relax, we can become more in tune with the voice of the Holy Spirit. 1 Kings 19:12 reads, "After the earthquake came a fire, but the Lord was not in the fire. And after the fire came a gentle whisper." The Spirit of God will not be audible unless your spirit is quiet enough to hear Him.

The Book of Psalm is filled with David's prayers which start with many disheartened, depressed and anxious words. In Psalm 38:6 and 8, he says, "I am hunched over, completely down; I wander around all day long, sad," "I'm worn out, completely crushed; I groan because of my miserable heart." (CEB) In Psalm 55:4-5, David is filled with anxiety as he cries out, "My heart pounds in my chest because death's terrors have reached me. Fear and trembling have come upon me; I'm shaking all over." (CEB)

In Matthew 11:28, Jesus says, "Come to me, all you who are weary and burdened, and I will give you rest." (NIV) And it is this very scripture that will be the center of the next meditation practice.

[3] *Anxiety Disorders. Accessed June 10, 2019 through https://anxiety.psych.ucla.edu/education*

[4] *What Causes Depression? Accessed June 10, 2019 through https://www.health.harvard.edu/mind-and-mood/what-causes-depression*

TECHNIQUE:

Quiet Waters Meditation (30 minutes)

In this 30-minute meditation, I will guide you through a visualization practice that will be centered around Matthew 11:28 along with a pranayama practice. The recording can be downloaded by going to my website, under the "Resources" tab (password protected):

https://www.jhenisolis.com/resources/quietwatersmeditation

(Password: **Psalm4610**)

JOURNALING PROMPTS:

1. What did you experience during the Quiet Waters meditation?

2. If you experienced any physical, mental or emotional discomforts during the meditation, were you able to acknowledge, accept, and surrender to stillness and peace?

3. Write down any spiritual insights you may have received from God, and find scriptures that confirm these insights.

Silent Meditation

For the next 20+ minutes, I invite you to begin your own silent meditation. Set the timer to the maximum time you'd like to meditate. Sit still, close your eyes, and begin with a gentle ujjayi pranayama practice. Choose one of the fruits of the spirits as your intention (love, joy, peace, patience, kindness, goodness, faithfulness, gentleness, or self-control). Do your best not to analyze; just experience this time of meditation, communing with God.

"The fruit of the Spirit is love, joy, peace, patience, kindness, goodness, faithfulness, gentleness, and self-control."

Galatians 5:22-23

JOURNALING PROMPTS:

1. What did you experience during your silent meditation?

2. If you experienced any physical, mental or emotional discomforts during the meditation, were you able to acknowledge, accept, and surrender to the intention that you set?

3. Write down any spiritual insights you may have received from God, and find scriptures that confirm these insights.

Epilogue

About 5 pages away from finishing up with writing this book, I was hit with a serious case of insecurities and fear. I found myself coming up with many reasons why I couldn't carve out time to finish writing this book. At the same time, I heard this voice in the back of my head telling me that this book was not ready for publishing. I started to experience self-doubt about whether or not anyone would even pick up this book.

It wasn't until I sat down, breathed and meditated on His promises that, *"...he who began a good work in [me] will carry it on to completion until the day of Christ Jesus,"* (Philippians 1:6) that I was able to *"take captive every thought to make it obedient to Christ."* (2 Corinthians 10:5b)

I had to go back to WHY I started writing this book in the first place: God put it on my heart to write this book in 2017, but I let my own insecurities stop me from doing so. For two years, I kept coming up with excuses as to why I was not qualified to write this book and why no one would buy it. I was right. I was NOT qualified, and I would not have been able to sell a single copy; because I had already decided that I couldn't do it, I really could not have done it. Then towards the end of 2018, God made it very clear (through my biblical meditations and through other people) that 2019 was the year for me to write this book out of pure obedience toward Him. So, I wrote this book, not being concerned with whether or not I felt I was qualified. It didn't matter to me whether I sold a million books or none because publishing this book was an act of obedience.

With everything we're faced with, we have the opportunity to take it to God in prayer with the goal of obeying what He reveals to us. When you incorporate biblical meditation into your times with God, your prayers become more intimate and your Bible-reading becomes more in-depth. Adding biblical meditation into your walk with God is sort of like adding fuel to an existing spark.

I pray that you were able to finish this book with a new sense of perspective and a deeper desire to obey our Father as He says in Psalm 46:10a,

"Be still, and know that I am God."

Additional Techniques

Everyday Pranayama Practice to Reduce Stress

1. Sit up tall with your spine in neutral.

2. Close your eyes and begin to breathe effortlessly and noiselessly.

3. Start counting down from 10 to 0, counting one down at each exhale:

   - Inhale, Exhale 10... Inhale, Exhale 9... so on and so forth until you reach 0.

   - Experience how your body feels heavier and more relaxed with each exhale.

   - If you lose count, start over again from 10.

4. Once you reach 0, inhale for four counts and exhale for four counts. Do this until you feel balanced and centered.

5. Now start counting from 0 to 10, counting one up at each inhale:

   - Inhale 0, Exhale... Inhale 1, Exhale... so on and so forth until you reach 10.

   - Experience how your body feels lighter and more energized with each inhale.

6. Once you reach 10, slowly open your eyes.

Incorporating Yoga Asanas into Your Quiet Times
(Psalm 139 Yoga Practice)

Here's a short Yoga practice using simple asanas (poses) as you recite Psalm 139:13-18 (the password-protected audio recording is available on my website in the Resources tab. Password: **Psalm4610**):

1. Place your hands and knees on the floor into Table Pose.
2. Inhale in Table Pose, then Exhale into Child's Pose.
3. Continue flowing from Table Pose to Child's Pose as you internally recite verse 13:

Table Pose: *For you created my inmost being*

Child's Pose: *You knit me together in my mother's womb.*

4. Inhale back to Table Pose and curl the toes under.

5. Exhale, lift the knees off the floor as you straighten your legs and lift the hips up and back into Downward Dog.

Table Pose

Downward Dog

6. Inhale as you lift your right leg up toward the sky, then exhale as you step the right foot forward.

One-Legged Downward Dog

7. Plant the back foot down as you inhale and rise up into Warrior 2.

Warrior 2

8. Stay in Warrior 2 as you internally recite Verse 14a. Continue to inhale and exhale (stay in the pose for 5-7 breaths):

Warrior 2:

I praise you because I am fearfully and wonderfully made

9. Inhale as you bring your left arm up to meet your right into Warrior 1 (adjust the feet placement as needed). Stay in this pose for 5-7 breaths as you internally recite Verse 14b:

Warrior 1:

Your works are wonderful, I know that full well.

10. Take another Inhale in Warrior 1 as you straighten your right leg. As you exhale, hinge at the hips as you fold forward into Pyramid Pose. Stay in this pose for 5-7 breaths as you internally recite Verse 15a:

Pyramid: *My frame was not hidden from you when I was made in the secret place…*

11. Inhale in Pyramid, and then step the left foot in to meet the right foot as you exhale. Stay folded in Folded Chair Pose for 5-7 breaths as you internally recite Verse 15b:

Folded Chair: *…when I was woven together in the depths of the earth.*

12. Inhale in Folded Chair Pose, and exhale as you step the left foot back.

13. Pivot both feet as you walk your hands over to the left foot so that you are in Pyramid Pose facing the other way.

14. Bend the left knee as you inhale and rise up into Warrior 2. Going back to Verses 14-15, internally recite Verse 14a again as you continue to inhale and exhale (stay in the pose for 5-7 breaths):

Warrior 2: *I praise you because I am fearfully and wonderfully made.*

15. Inhale as you bring your right arm up to meet your left into Warrior 1 (adjust the feet placement as needed). Stay in this pose for 5-7 breaths as you internally recite Verse 14b:

Warrior 1: Your works are wonderful, I know that full well.

16. Take another Inhale in Warrior 1, and as you exhale, hinge at the hips as you fold forward into Pyramid Pose. Stay in this pose for 5-7 breaths as you internally recite Verse 15a:

Pyramid: *My frame was not hidden from you when I was made in the secret place...*

17. Inhale in Pyramid, and then step the left foot in to meet the right foot as you exhale. Stay folded in Folded Chair Pose for 5-7 breaths as you internally recite Verse 15b:

...when I was woven together in the depths of the earth

18.　Inhale, look forward as you straighten your legs, straighten the back with straight arms and fingertips on the floor Internally recite Verse 16a:

Half Forward Fold: *Your eyes saw my unformed body...*

19.　Exhale and Inhale as you bend your knees and come all the way up to standing in Mountain Pose. Gaze up to the sky as you internally recite Verses 16b-17:

...all the days ordained for me were written in your book before one of them came to be. How precious to me are your thoughts, God! How vast is the sum of them!

20. Exhale as you bring your hands to heart and close your eyes; Internally recite Verse 18a:

Were I to count them, they would outnumber the grains of sand...

21. Slowly open your eyes as you internally recite Verse 18b:

...when I awake, I am still with you.

Scripture References

The following list contains the NIV Bible passages where I made a mention of specific scriptures but did not write out the verse(s) within the chapters.

Prologue

Psalm 46:10

"He says, "Be still, and know that I am God; I will be exalted among the nations, I will be exalted in the earth."

Chapter 1

Matthew 12:44-45

"Then it says, 'I will return to the house I left.' When it arrives, it finds the house unoccupied, swept clean and put in order. Then it goes and takes with it seven other spirits more wicked than itself, and they go in and live there. And the final condition of that person is worse than the first. That is how it will be with this wicked generation."

Joshua 1:8

"Keep this Book of the Law always on your lips; meditate on it day and night, so that you may be careful to do everything written in it. Then you will be prosperous and successful."

Psalm 1:1-2	*"Blessed is the one who does not walk in step with the wicked or stand in the way that sinners take or sit in the company of mockers, but whose delight is in the law of the LORD, and who meditates on his law day and night."*

Psalm 104:34	"May my meditation be pleasing to him, as I rejoice in the Lord."

Chapter 4:

Romans 7:21-25	*"So I find this law at work: Although I want to do good, evil is right there with me. For in my inner being I delight in God's law; but I see another law at work in me, waging war against the law of my mind and making me a prisoner of the law of sin at work within me. What a wretched man I am! Who will rescue me from this body that is subject to death? Thanks be to God, who delivers me through Jesus Christ our Lord!" So then, I myself in my mind am a slave to God's law, but in my sinful nature[a] a slave to the law of sin."*

Psalm 139:13-14   *"For you created my inmost being;*
you knit me together in my mother's
womb. I praise you because I am
fearfully and wonderfully made;
your works are wonderful, I know
that full well."

Philippians 2:3-4   *"Do nothing out of selfish ambition*
or vain conceit, but in humility
consider others better than
yourselves. Each of you should look
not only to your own interests, but
also to the interests of others."

2 Peter 3:9   *"The Lord is not slow in keeping his*
promise, as some understand
slowness. Instead he is patient with
you, not wanting anyone to perish,
but everyone to come to
repentance."

Philippians 4:7   *"And the peace of God, which*
transcends all understanding, will
guard your hearts and your minds in
Christ Jesus."

Philippians 2:1-4   *"Therefore if you have any*
encouragement from being united
with Christ, if any comfort from his
love, if any common sharing in the

Spirit, if any tenderness and compassion, then make my joy complete by being like-minded, having the same love, being one in spirit and of one mind. Do nothing out of selfish ambition or vain conceit. Rather, in humility value others above yourselves, not looking to your own interests but each of you to the interests of the others."

Romans 12:15

"Rejoice with those who rejoice; mourn with those who mourn."

Galatians 6:2

"Carry each other's burdens, and in this way you will fulfill the law of Christ."

Matthew 5:7

"Blessed are the merciful, for they will be shown mercy."

Chapter 5:

Romans 5:3-5

"Not only that, but we also rejoice in our sufferings, because we know that suffering produces perseverance; perseverance, character; and character, hope. And hope does not disappoint us,

because God has poured out His love into our hearts through the Holy Spirit, whom He has given us." (BSB)

Romans 12:12   *"Be joyful in hope, patient in affliction, persistent in prayer."* (BSB)

Psalm 32:5   *"I acknowledged my sin to You, and my iniquity I did not hide; I said, "I will confess my transgressions to the LORD"; and You forgave the guilt of my sin."*

James 5:16   *"Therefore confess your sins to each other and pray for each other so that you may be healed. The prayer of a righteous person is powerful and effective."*

James 5:16   *"Therefore confess your sins to each other and pray for each other so that you may be healed. The prayer of a righteous person is powerful and effective."*